N. Singh

Hardcover ISBN: 978-81-960160-6-7
Paperback ISBN: 978-81-960160-8-1
eBook ISBN: 978-81-960160-7-4

©Publisher

Publisher: Pharos Books (P) Ltd.
Plot No.-55, Main Mother Dairy Road
Pandav Nagar, East Delhi-110092
Phone: 011-40395855, +4049916623
WhatsApp: +91 8368220032
E-mail: sales@pharosbooks.in
Website: www.pharosbooks.in
First Edition: 2023

I AM I CAN
By N. SINGH

"Believe you can and you're halfway there."

—*Theodore Roosevelt*

About this book

I have written this book for everyone— young and old, men, women, students, educators, business people, administrators, parents, homemakers, sports enthusiasts, entertainers— yes, and you!

I guarantee that if you read the material carefully and apply what you learn, you'll notice big changes taking place within two or three months, and a year from now you'll look back amazed at how much more confident you've become.

Preface

Confidence does not come in fixed amounts— it varies from place to place, moment to moment according to what you're doing and with whom. For example, some people are extremely confident at work but fail in their relationships; and many brilliant individuals can barely string two words together when away from the security of their offices or laboratories.

How about you?

Take a close look at yourself.

Step back and observe.

If you're struggling like I did most of my life, this book is the one-stop introduction and solution to all the problems concerning confidence that needs to be addressed. As a child and then a young adult I too was not very confident about how I looked, how I spoke and how I behaved. But that soon changed when I started consciously acting on how I thought, behaved and felt. With this book, I hope you'd able to do the same.

Author

CONTENTS

Life is not easy for any of us. But what of that? We must have perseverance and above all confidence in ourselves. We must believe that we are gifted for something and that this thing must be attained."

—Marie Curie

1 Introduction

When you envision a confident person, you might think of someone who takes big, bold actions, like running for office or giving the next TED Talk. But there can be a lot of boldness and bravery in small steps. Confidence isn't something you have to possess every moment of every day. Nor should you expect to jump instantly into perfect self-assurance tomorrow. Instead, confidence is a choice to take steps to act in line with your values.

Confident people are usually:

- Flexible

- Unafraid to be wrong

- Have faith that they can deliver on their promises

- Ask for help when needed.

- Are not easily thrown off by setbacks but instead see them as challenges to learn from

People with low confidence face an uphill battle. When your confidence is low you tend to become more reserved and refrain from taking any action that would seem untoward. It's much easier to remain in the safe confines of the status quo and not expose yourself to the possibility of failure or rejection. The world is awash with competition and ambition, in everything from getting a job to getting a date. If you are a reserved individual and hesitate or fail to convince others of your positive attributes there will always be someone else ready to take what could be yours. This is true everywhere— with recreational sports teams, the workplace, and relationships. Low confidence tends to immobilize us. Those lacking self-esteem are more likely to experience depression, anxiety, problem anger, chronic pain, immunosuppression, and a variety of other distressing physical and psychological symptoms.

There's a reason your confidence has taken a hit. It could be a genuine reason, like recently breaking up with your partner or suffering from acute shyness. Or it could be some relatively minor event from the past that no longer applies to you—but it has grown so much in your mind that it keeps filling your mind with negative thoughts.

Either way, your immediate or distant past doesn't define you now or your future potential. Change and growth are always possible when you're motivated and determined, regardless of your past, your personality, or your self-perceptions. If you want to be confident, you can be—if you're willing to take action. And not just one action or a few actions, but repeated actions until fear and doubt no longer have a grip on you.

All success begins with thinking and culminates in action. It is possible action will result in failure, but inaction always leads to nothing—guaranteed. An essential component of confidence is the ability to be comfortable with the uncertainty of action and the sting of failure. Failure will happen on occasion. Sometimes it happens many times.

The fear of failure and rejection is the only thing standing between you and your confidence. The only way to beat that fear is to take action. Take action now, and become the person you want to be.

‘It feels really good to do something for myself.’

One person who was motivated to change was Aarti. She had lived by other people's rules for most of her life, usually allowing others to make decisions on her behalf. Then one evening, after a heated row, her abusive and manipulative husband of 20 years stormed out in a rage, threatening to leave her. He expected her to beg him to return, as she had always done before. But it came as a shock to him that she had been quietly working on her confidence and this time she refused. At first, he threatened, then he pleaded, but she held firm. This was the beginning of a new phase in her life. Six months later, no longer facing the daily outbursts which she had previously endured, her home was a haven of calm. She had taken computing lessons, found a well-paid job, enrolled in evening makeup classes, and was practicing at a local salon. Even her son no longer had to endure the tension and was happier and more settled at school. 'Since I worked on my confidence,' Aarti said, 'I feel as if I'm in control. It feels really good to do something for myself that I've always wanted to do. And I know if I don't I've only got myself to blame.'

"If you have no confidence in self, you are twice defeated in the race of life. With confidence, you have won even before you have started."

—Cicero

2   Understanding Confidence

"What lies behind us and what lies before us are tiny matters compared to what lies within us."

—Ralph Waldo Emerson

One's confidence stems from their self-esteem. If you see yourself as someone capable, you will be full of confidence to do anything. It is built on an appreciative opinion of oneself. It is the conviction that you are as worthwhile as anyone else. It is not being self-centred, overconfident or arrogant, but feeling that you have an intrinsic value.

Confidence has three constituents:

1. Intrinsic Worth

A basic premise is that all people have equal, immeasurable, unchanging intrinsic worth as a person. Worth as a person is neither earned nor increased or diminished by external factors, such as the way people treat you, bad decisions, or fluctuations in your social or monetary status.

2. Receive Love

Love does not create worth. However, love helps us experience our worth. Children with confidence tend to have parents who love them. These parents show interest in the children's lives, care for them, and encourage and support them. Even though we might not always have the love of others, we can always choose to love ourselves.

3. Growth

We tend to feel better about ourselves when we are living constructively—making sensible decisions, evolving required attributes, and polishing our rough edges—simply, growing. Growing does not change our core worth, but it helps us to experience it with greater satisfaction.

Self-Confidence vs. Insecurity

When learning how to be more confident, it can be helpful to understand how someone with self-confidence is different from someone insecure. Here are just some of the differences between the two:

Confident People

- Celebrate other people's success
- Open-minded
- Optimistic
- Willing to take risks
- Laugh at themselves
- Decisive
- Always learning and growing
- Admit mistakes
- Accept responsibility

Insecure People

- Judge and are jealous of others
- Close-minded
- Pessimistic
- Afraid of change
- Hide flaws
- Indecisive
- Act like a know-it-all
- Make excuses
- Blame others

Benefits of Self-Confidence

Being confident in yourself just feels good. That said, having self-confidence can also bring many additional benefits at home, at work, and within your relationships. Here's a look at a few of the positive effects of learning how to be confident:

- **Better performance:** Rather than waste time and energy worrying that you aren't good enough, you can devote your energy to your efforts. Ultimately, you'll perform better when you have more self-confidence.

- **Healthier relationships:** Having self-confidence not only impacts how you feel about yourself, but it helps you better understand and love others. It also gives you the strength to walk away from a relationship if you're not getting what you want or deserve.

- **Openness to try new things:** When you believe in yourself, you're more willing to try new things. Whether you apply for a promotion or sign up for a cooking class, putting yourself out there is a lot easier when you have confidence in yourself and your abilities.

- **Resilience:** Believing in yourself can enhance your resilience or ability to bounce back from any challenges or adversities you face in life.

☞ **REMEMBER**

➢ Confidence is a sense of satisfaction that comes from recognizing and appreciating our existing worth and then choosing to love and grow.

➢ Confidence is not comparative and competitive.

➢ Confidence does not boast or put others down.

➢ Confidence can be built through persistent effort.

➢ The building process is one that involves seeing clearly, loving, and developing.

Believe in yourself! Have faith in your abilities! Without a humble but reasonable confidence in your own powers you cannot be successful or happy."

—Norman Vincent Peale

3   The Theory behind Building Confidence

In building confidence, effective attempts target thoughts, feelings, and behaviours.

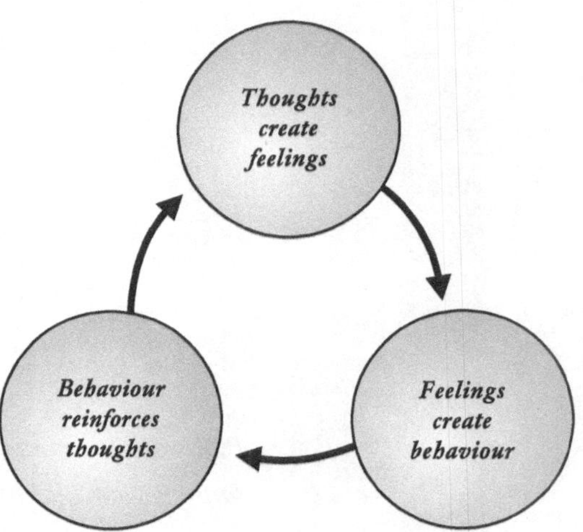

Acknowledge Your Thoughts

The Theravada Buddhist tradition believes that we are of two minds: the wisdom mind and the ordinary mind. The wisdom mind represents our true happy nature, which is the domain of our intrinsic value. Whereas, the ordinary mind attaches to unsettled thoughts and disturbing negative emotions.

Unreasonably negative thoughts prevent us from enjoying our true happy nature. And what we think, good or bad, depends on a number of factors:

- Our social environment

- Our physical condition

- Our coping skills

- Our behavioural patterns

When these negative thoughts occur we can fight, flee, or allow them. When we fight, we tense up, and the tensing itself tends to increase arousal and pain. Another option is to flee by avoiding, sedating, dissociating, wishing problems away, or asking why. None of these approaches is effective in the long run. But when we **allow,** we stop struggling with our challenges and simply hold them in kind awareness. As we stop struggling and trying to fix problems, we gain a different perspective, inner peace and confidence that we can handle life, and liberation from our attachments to negative thoughts and feelings. Switch your thoughts and you automatically alter your emotions and redirect your actions.

Becoming Aware of Your Feelings

The most basic indicators of your confidence are your emotions. The more aware you are of emotional signals, the more you will be able to move your feelings from negative to positive and can build confidence in yourself. Recognize the physical sensations that accompany your emotions. For example, you may feel anxious butterflies in your stomach or excited tingles down your spine. Register the different responses that you have to your emotions—perhaps losing your temper when you feel irritated, or being more generous than usual when contented.

Once you've learned which situations affect your self-esteem, notice your feelings about them. This includes what you tell yourself (self-talk) and how you view the situations. Now replace negative or manipulated/created feelings (because of societal constructs) with positive ones. Try these strategies:

- **Forgive yourself.** Everyone makes mistakes. But mistakes aren't permanent reflections on you as a person. They're moments in time. Tell yourself, "I made a mistake, but that doesn't make me a bad person."

- **Use hopeful statements.** Be kind and encouraging to yourself. Instead of thinking a situation won't go well, focus on the positive. Tell yourself, "Even though it's tough, I can handle this."

- **Consider what you've learned.** If it was a negative experience, what changes can you make next time to create a more positive outcome?

- **Relabel upsetting thoughts.** Think of negative thoughts as signals to try new, healthy patterns. Ask yourself, "What can I think and do to make this less stressful?"

- **Encourage yourself.** Give yourself credit for making positive changes. For example, "My presentation might not have been perfect, but my colleagues asked questions and remained engaged. That means I met my goal."

- **Focus on the positive.** Think about the parts of your life that work well. Remember the skills you've used to cope with challenges.

Behave Yourself

If you're aiming to develop your inner confidence, then you must accept the fact that confidence is the byproduct of consistently implementing a set of actions and behaviours that create self-worth. These actions and behaviours will cause your character to transform and you will become a more confident version of yourself because you have increased your perception of yourself.

You must give up these three behaviours in order to create new levels of confidence:

1. Eliminate Negative Self-Talk

Most of what we suffer from, emotionally and mentally, comes from how we talk to ourselves in our own head; this is called negative self-talk. Whatever you believe in will happen. So you really only have one of two choices to make.

If you want a positive outlook on life, then you must have positive thoughts about how you view yourself. We must view ourselves as powerful beings who are capable of achieving anything we choose to achieve.

2. Stop Doubting Yourself

Self-doubt is part of our daily life and what we experience every day. There are many cases where even a little self-doubt can become dangerous. If you keep ignoring that fear, it will fuel your self-doubt and will drive you off the road to progress.

This is the biggest energy leak ever and only forms in our minds because we are not putting in the work that is required for making new progress. Remember that the work we put in instills our self-worth. Lack of it puts doubt in our minds. If you are struggling to make progress in one area of life, consider developing progress and creating success in another area, as this will help eliminate your self-doubt. Also, remember that you cannot solve a self-doubt or self-belief problem while you still have the same negative mindset that created that self-doubt.

3. Crush Your Fear of Failure

If you fear failing, you will. If you picture winning, you win. We literally become what we visualize. The fear of failing has been so instilled in us while growing up that we never want to feel it again. This fear of failure results in us unconsciously sabotaging our own chances of success, and we will do whatever it takes to not make any forward progress. It's time to stop thinking about what others think of you if you fail. It is also critical not to attach failure to being incapable.

The Four-Step Method

Negative thinking can quickly spiral out of control and destroy your confidence if you allow it. This is where The Four Step Method– a simple technique for becoming aware of disempowering thoughts – comes in. It's quickly learned and easily applied and, with practice, soon becomes second nature.

The four steps are:
1. **Be mindful.**
2. **Stop disempowering thoughts.**
3. **Replace them with empowering thoughts.**
4. **Keep going until it becomes automatic.**

The Four Step Method is the most effective technique for building self-confidence.

☞ REMEMBER

- ➢ You need to distinguish your feelings, thoughts, and beliefs.
- ➢ A positive thought creates a positive feeling, and motivates positive action.
- ➢ Your feelings, thoughts, and beliefs can be shifted from negative to positive.
- ➢ A positive belief influences your whole approach to life.

"Your success will be determined by your own confidence and fortitude."

—*Michelle Obama*

4. How to Be More Confident

Fortunately, there are several ways you can increase your self-confidence. Whether you lack confidence in one specific area or struggle to feel confident about anything, these nine confidence boosters can help.

1. Stop Comparing Yourself to Others

Do you compare your looks to the people you follow on Instagram? Or maybe you compare your salary to what your friend earns. Social comparison theory explains that comparisons are natural. But it probably won't help boost your confidence.

It can even have the opposite effect. When people compare themselves to others, they feel envy. And the more jealous they are, the worse they feel. How do you build confidence when you find yourself making comparisons? First, remember that this isn't helpful. Everyone has their own race and **life is not a competition**. When you're jealous of someone else's life, it's also helpful to remember your own strengths and accomplishments.

> **Tip:** Keep a gratitude journal to better remember areas of life where you've been blessed. This can help you focus on your own life instead of the lives of others.

2. Surround Yourself With Positive People

Take a moment and think about how your friends make you feel. Do they lift you up or do they knock you down? Do they constantly judge you or accept you for who you are? The people you spend time with can influence your thoughts and attitudes about yourself, perhaps more than you realize. So pay attention to how others make you feel.

If you feel bad after dating a certain person, it may be time to say goodbye. Instead, surround yourself with people who love you and want the best for you. Look for other people who are positive and can help you build your confidence. Confidence and a positive attitude go hand in hand.

3. Take Care of Your Body

It is hard to feel good when you're abusing your body. When you take care of yourself, you know you're doing something positive for your mind, body, and spirit, and it will naturally make you feel more confident.

Here are some self-care practices associated with higher levels of self-care:

- **Nutrition:** Eating a healthy diet has many benefits, including a higher level of confidence and self-esteem. When you fuel your body with nutrient-dense foods, you feel healthier, stronger, and more energetic, which can make you feel better.

- **Exercise:** Studies consistently show that physical exercise builds confidence. Regular physical activity improves body image. And when your body image improves, you'll feel more confident.

- **Meditation:** Meditation helps you to know and accept yourself. It also teaches you to stop negative self-talk and shut out useless mental chatter that hurts your confidence.

- **Sleep:** Lack of sleep can affect your emotions.In contrast, good sleep quality has been associated with positive personality traits such as optimism and self-esteem.

Taking care of yourself is important for self-confidence. Make sure you get what you need to be comfortable with yourself and your abilities.

4. Be Kind to Yourself

Self-compassion means treating yourself kindly when you make a mistake, fail, or experience a setback. It allows you to be more emotionally flexible, helping you to better manage challenging emotions and improve your connection with yourself and others.

You need to practice positive self-talk. Negative self-talk can limit your abilities and lower your confidence by convincing your subconscious that you "can't handle" something, or that it's "too hard" and that you "shouldn't even try." Optimism, on the other hand, can encourage self-compassion and help you overcome doubts and embrace new challenges.

Here are some examples of how to challenge pessimistic self-talk and shift your thoughts into a more positive mindset, which will boost your confidence:

- "I can't handle this" or "This is impossible" becomes "I can do this" or "I just have to try."

- "I can't do anything right" becomes "I can do better" Time" or "At least I learned something ."

- "I hate public speaking" becomes "I don't like public speaking" and "Everyone has strengths and weaknesses."

5. Face Your Fears

Stop procrastinating until you feel more confident, such as —asking someone out on a date or asking for a promotion. One of the best ways to build confidence in these situations is to face your fears head-on.

Practice facing some of your fears that result from a lack of self-confidence. If you're afraid of embarrassing yourself or think you're going to screw up, try anyway. A little doubt can even help improve performance. Tell yourself it's just an experiment and see what happens.

You might learn that being a little scared or making a few mistakes isn't as bad as you thought. And every time you advance, you gain more confidence. Ultimately, this can help deter you from taking risks that lead to serious negative consequences.

6. Do Things You're Good At

What happens when you do things that you are good at? Your self-confidence starts to soar. Your strengths become even stronger, which helps improve your belief in yourself.

If you're good at a certain sport, for instance, make it a point to train or play at least once a week. If you're good at a particular task at work, try to do that task more often. Building on your strengths can also help you build your self-confidence.

IDENTIFY YOUR STRENGTHS

To get started, jot down some notes answering the prompts below:

◊ Compliments I've received:

1.

2.

3.

◊ An important role I've fulfilled:

◊ An important task I've tackled:

◊ Skills I enjoy using regardless of the task:

1.

2.

3.

◊ A time I've helped someone else:

When you're done, read over what you've written and try to notice them.

List three or more of your strengths below.

1.

2.

3.

7. Know When to Say No

While doing things you're good at can give your self-confidence a boost, it's equally important to recognize situations that can cause your confidence to plummet. Maybe you find that every time you participate in a certain activity, you feel worse about yourself instead of better.

Saying no to activities that tend to zap your self-confidence is okay. Certainly, you don't want to avoid doing anything that makes you feel uncomfortable because discomfort is often part of the personal growth process. At the same time, there's nothing wrong with knowing your boundaries and sticking to them.

Setting social and emotional boundaries enables you to feel safer psychologically. It can also help you feel more in control. Self-confidence is, in part, feeling like you have control over your life. Boundaries help establish this feeling of control.

The next time someone suggests doing something that you know will lower your self-confidence, respectfully decline. You don't have to avoid that activity forever either. Once you learn how to be more confident, you may feel strong enough to try it again—without hurting the confidence you have in yourself.

8. Set Realistic Goals

Pursuing your goals often involves failing several times until you figure out what works. This can make you wonder if you have what it takes to succeed. It can also leave you questioning how to be more confident while still achieving your dreams. The answer lies in setting realistic goals.

Setting high-reaching goals and failing to achieve them has been found to damage confidence levels. Conversely, realistic goals are achievable. And the more you achieve your goals, the greater your confidence in yourself and your abilities.

> **Tip:** To set realistic goals, write down what you want to achieve. Next, ask yourself what chance you have of attaining it. (Be honest!) If the answer is slim to none, the goal may be a bit too lofty. Dial it back so it is more realistic and achievable.

"No one can make you feel inferior without your consent."

—Eleanor Roosevelt

5

It's Time for Action

"Stay afraid, but do it anyway. What's important is the action. You don't have to wait to be confident. Just do it and eventually the confidence will follow."

—Carrie Fisher

Action is the cure for low confidence. Unfortunately, low self-confidence tends to immobilize us. Change and growth are always possible when you are motivated and determined, regardless of your background, personality or self-image. Your immediate or distant past does not define you now or your potential future. If you want to be confident, you can be if you're ready to take action. And not just one action or a few actions, but repeated actions until fear and doubt no longer control you. And remember that every success begins with a thought and culminates in action. It is possible action will result in failure, but inaction always leads to nothing—guaranteed.

Add Confidence To every ION of your being

Now let us look at various areas; you act on these and you are 90% there! Take small and manageable actions to kick-start your confidence. You may not lack confidence in all of these areas, but the actions can further cement your existing confidence and provide skills you can utilize for situations that arise in the future.

1. Communication

Whether at work, in your love life, or with friends and family, good communication fosters better understanding, helps us resolve differences, promotes mutual trust and respect, and allows creative ideas to flourish.

Although communication seems fairly simple and straightforward, so much of our communication is misunderstood or misinterpreted. This can cause conflict and wounded feelings in personal and professional relationships, which demoralises our confidence.

One of the most positive things you can do for your confidence is to learn the skills of healthy, confident communication in your personal and professional life and to put those skills into practice.

→ Actions to take:

- **Think before you speak.** When you're nervous or lack confidence, you can sometimes lose the filter between your brain and mouth. You blurt things out without thinking them through. Or you might be in a rush to "say it and get it over with" before you lose your nerve. By considering and organizing your thoughts in advance, you can save yourself from embarrassment or prevent offending someone else.

- **Avoid using filler words in conversations.** These are little sounds like, "um," "er," and "ah," that we use when trying to think of the next thing we want to say. Sometimes we use them because we're nervous and our thoughts escape us. A conversation, presentation, or speech littered with fillers makes the speaker appear unprepared or disengaged.

- **Pay attention to pitch, tone, and speed.** The pitch of your voice does make an impact on those who hear you, and they make value judgments based on how you sound. Speaking in a high voice gives the impression you're nervous and lack confidence. A lower-pitched voice tends to be calming and persuasive. When you speak too quickly, people can't understand you and begin to tune out and stop listening.

- **Know what you are talking about.** Genuine preparation is key to feeling confident, especially in communication. Whether you're having a discussion with a friend about politics or making a presentation, you'll feel much more self-assured if you know your facts and have thoroughly prepared.

2. Appearance

One of the main sources of low confidence for nearly everyone relates to appearance. Although most of the population is average looking compared to what you see on social media/media, everyone still obsesses about obtaining that ideal. In obsessing about that "perfect body", that "perfect look", we undermine the way we look. And when you do that o yourself how can you expect your confidence to soar high?

The key to confidence in your appearance is self-acceptance. Acceptance of yourself as you really are—with all the flaws. When you develop a positive self-image, you cultivate confidence in the person you are. So to develop this positive image of yourself you need to start acting now!

→ Actions to take:

- **Focus on your best.** We tend to focus on our flaws and bypass our positive qualities. But what if you let your flaws fade into the background and allowed those attractive features to move to the forefront of your attention? Focusing on your best is a conscious choice to improve your confidence.

- **Improve what you can.** Self-acceptance doesn't mean you shouldn't make positive changes when you can, especially if it improves your confidence and self-esteem. Dressing well, wearing make-up properly, and getting an updated haircut will make you more self-assured and show others that you feel good about yourself. Even maintaining your health, and hygiene and grooming yourself like exercising regularly, keeping your hair clean, your nails trimmed or manicured, your face shaved and your clothes neat and unwrinkled, will give you an immediate boost of confidence.

- **Use the mirror technique.** Stand before a full-length mirror, completely naked, without the use of any complementary lighting, makeup, etc. As you gaze over your face and body, make note of your feelings and thoughts. You'll find some aspects of your face and body are harder to look at than others. These aspects have acquired such negative power in your mind that they might impact self-esteem and confidence. As you focus on these parts, look in the mirror and repeat out loud, "I completely accept and love myself as I am, whatever my imperfections may be." The mirror technique is effective in helping foster self-acceptance related to your physical appearance and learning to love yourself completely for who and what you are regardless of your flaws.

3. Body Language

A large percentage of how people perceive you comes from body language. This includes posture, gestures, facial expressions, and eye movements. Your body language might reveal your true feelings or intentions.

Understanding and managing body language boosts your confidence in two ways. First, by managing your body language and sending apt signals in particular situations, you receive positive feedback and feel assured you aren't damaging your own success or the perceptions of others. Secondly and more importantly, when you practice powerful, positive body language, you are sending messages to your brain to reinforce positive, confident feelings. Confident body language truly makes you feel more confident.

→ Actions to take:

- **Practice smiling.** Smiling not only makes you more attractive and trustworthy, but it also improves your health, your stress level, and your feelings about yourself. Smiling slows the heart and relaxes the body, and it releases endorphins that counteract and diminish stress hormones. It also has been shown to increase productivity while performing tasks.

- **Pay attention to posture.** Good posture reflects a confident demeanour to others. When you stand straight, with your shoulders back and head held high, you look self-assured and poised.

- **Remember your arms and legs.** Crossing your arms suggests you feel defensive, self-protective, and closed off. Crossing your legs away from another person can suggest you dislike them or feel discomfort. Crossing your ankles can signal you're holding something back. Hands clasped and crossed over the genitals is a self-comfort gesture that reveals vulnerability or shyness. Tapping your fingers and fidgeting tells others you are bored, impatient, or frustrated.

- **Have a strong handshake.** A firm handshake is a universal sign of confidence, and everyone, including women, should have one. A handshake should be strong, but not crushing, offered with a cool dry hand and a few up-and-down shakes, as well as a few seconds of eye contact. It is a sign of mutual respect from both parties and makes a great first impression.

- **Stop fidgeting.** Fidgeting, like shaking your foot, twirling your hair, or biting your nails, is an obvious sign of anxiety and nervousness. These nervous movements draw attention away from what you're saying and distract people from your message. Avoid touching your face or neck which also indicates you feel anxious. Fidgeting sends the message that you are not self-assured.

- **Practice appropriate eye contact.** Eye contact suggests you're truthful, engaging, and approachable. It communicates a sense of intimacy and confidence and makes the other person feel more positive and connected to you. However, too much eye contact can send the signal you're aggressive or maybe even a little strange.

> **Tip:** If you want to reach an agreement, win the girl, or persuade someone to your side of things, engaged body language gives you more confidence and sends powerful messages to others to win them over. Engaged body language involves using open gestures, smiling and nodding, and mirroring the expressions and movements of the other person. Once you've reached your goal, seal the deal by offering a firm handshake, saying "thank you", and using good posture.

"Don't wait until everything is just right. It will never be perfect. There will always be challenges, obstacles and less than perfect conditions. So what? Get started now. With each step you take, you will grow stronger and stronger, more and more skilled, more and more self-confident, and more and more successful."

—*Mark Victor Hansen*

6

Self-Improvement

Those not inclined toward self-examination may never realize something needs fixing until it is broken. Sometimes the areas where we are weakest are the places we need to focus the most attention. It is through a desire to become a better, more actualized person mentally, physically, and emotionally, that we feel increasingly confident in ourselves.

Enhancing your own value or worth and becoming the best version of yourself takes intentional work. You can do these for the same:

1. **Learn a new skill**

Learning a new skill, especially a challenging skill you're unfamiliar with, can improve your mental sharpness, advance your career opportunities, and boost your confidence. Through continued learning, you develop a deeper understanding and knowledge in areas that interest you.

2. **Improve your EQ**

Your emotional intelligence quotient is made up of four core skills: self-awareness, self-management, social awareness, and relationship management. When we boost our EQ, we improve our interactions and relationships in all settings. A higher EQ affords more self-control, helps you navigate conflict, and makes you a better communicator. All of these outcomes build your confidence, as you see the positive results of a sharpened EQ.

3. **Set goals**

There's no doubt that setting goals increase your chance of success and the frequency of your success. Setting a goal is the first and most important step toward any achievement. Both the actions toward and the achievement of your goal will boost your confidence. With every step forward, you feel empowered and motivated to continue. With every accomplishment, you'll believe more and more in your capacity for success. But beware, as we discussed earlier, your goals should not be unrealistic.

4. **Break some bad habits**

Our bad habits influence confidence. These habits harm our health, relationships, career success, or financial security. The resulting problems further deteriorate our confidence. Bad habits are hard to break, especially physical addictions, like smoking. They require much more than desire and willpower. Once you learn the skills involved in breaking bad habits, you'll get an immediate confidence boost knowing you finally have the tools to drop the habit. Once the habit is gone, you'll see a surge of improvements in other areas of your life, shooting your confidence even further.

5. Create life balance

Having a balanced life means you manage the various elements in your life without feeling your heart or mind tugged in any specific direction. You know exactly how much time you want to devote to work, family, learning, tasks, friends, free time, and other important elements of your life. You understand the value of physical, mental, and emotional balance as well, and create ways to find balance in these aspects of your life as well. Having balance reduces stress and confusion, and frees you up to pursue those priorities that support your confidence and well-being.

> **Tip:** Don't forget to monitor your progress! It is the best way to reach your goals, big or small. Try to quantify your accomplishments: the number of applications you're submitting to jobs or graduate schools, what you're eating and how much you're exercising, write down whatever your goal may be. It will help you stay on course, and you will build confidence as you see the progress you're making in real-time.

MINI CONFIDENCE BOOSTERS

Use these quick "hype-up" strategies ahead of a big day to boost your confidence.

- **A favourite outfit:** If you have an outfit that makes you feel like a million bucks, by all means, wear it when you're facing your biggest confidence challenges. Oddly, this works even if you're going into a phone interview where no one will see you.

- **A playlist:** Listening to your favourite confidence-boosting anthems can be a big help as you're going through your morning routine on a stressful day. It's a bonus if they make you want to dance around your bathroom and sing along, working through those nerves!

- **A reward:** If you're trying to push yourself to do something scary, it can help to promise yourself a little reward: "If I ask Raina on a date, I'll buy myself an ice cream cone afterwards." If you tie the reward to your effort rather than the outcome, it will remind you that action itself is more important than success.

- **A role model:** Picture someone you know who comes off as confident but not arrogant or pushy. You'll often find you can emulate that person's fearlessness for a moment.

- **A confidence buddy:** Telling a friend ahead of time that you're committing to taking a certain step will help ensure that you do it.

"Hi Varun, I'll go to the gym starting tomorrow."
"Are you sure, Arjun?"
"Yes of course! I bet on it!"
The next day arrives. Arjun is lethargic. He doesn't want to get out of his bed. Yet, he goes to the gym the next day because he had told Varun about it.

▶ **ACTIVITY**

This activity is to gauge how someone feels about themselves. If you score on the low end, that might mean you need to practice more self-love or self-compassion.

Answer the following questions with **"most of the time,"** **"some of the time,"** or **"almost never."**

1. My feelings get easily hurt.

2. I get upset if someone criticizes me, even if they mean well and offer constructive criticism.

3. I get angry at myself if I make a small mistake, even if it is an honest one.

4. I typically ask other people what they think I should do, instead of making my own decisions.

5. I typically go along with the group, even if I don't necessarily agree.

6. I am uncomfortable when accepting compliments.

7. I don't feel like I measure up or feel good enough.

8. It's common for me to self-criticize or say negative things about myself, like telling myself I am stupid, fat, or just no good.

9. When I look in the mirror, I don't like what I see and don't feel attractive.

10. I find myself apologizing for things all of the time, even for things that aren't my fault.

If you answered "almost never" for most of the questions, you have healthy self-esteem. Everyone has times when they feel down, but as long as you don't feel like that every day, you will be fine.

If you answered "most of the time" to many of the questions, you may need to take some additional steps to boost your self-esteem. This doesn't necessarily mean you are depressed; it just means you may be a little too hard on yourself.

If you answered "some of the time" to many of the questions, you could still benefit from practising a little self-compassion and self-love.

"Confidence doesn't come out of nowhere. It's a result of something ... hours and days and weeks and years of constant work and dedication."

—*Roger Staubach*

7   Boost Confidence with Yoga

Changing your posture will not only radically shift how you move, but also transform how you feel and present yourself to others. Over time your shy and slouchy posture will shift into one that's more powerful—with your shoulders drawn back and your core shining ahead.

Here are 11 yoga poses that will help build and present a confident you:

1. Balasana (Child's Pose)

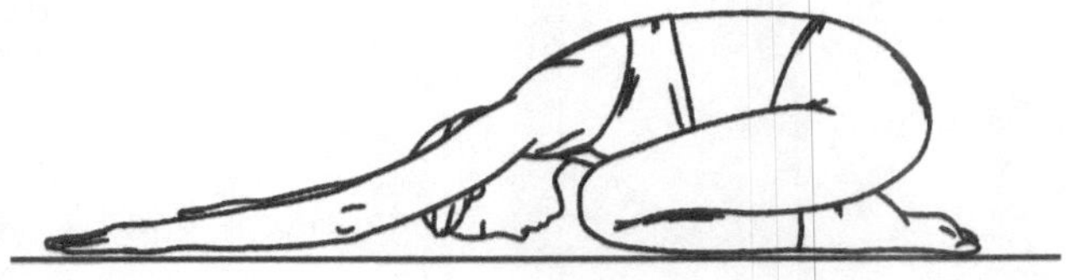

Start with your knees slightly wider than your rib cage with your big toes touching. Let your sacrum relax toward your heels, and stretch your arms forward with your palms facing up. After a few breaths, interlace your fingers and wrap your triceps under and down to create space in your shoulders and neck. With your elbows rooted to the mat, reach your knuckles back toward the nape of your neck. Stay here for 1-2 minutes.

2. Adho Mukha Svanasana (Downward-Facing Dog Pose)

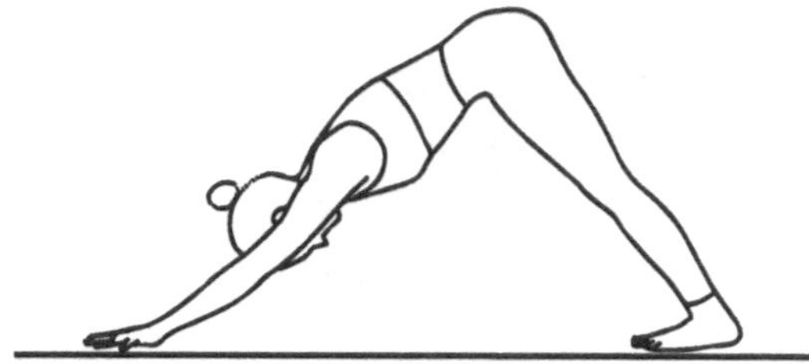

Come forward with your wrists under your shoulders and your knees under your hips. Spread your fingers wide, then tuck your toes under, pressing your legs up and back to Downward-Facing Dog Pose. Make sure your feet are hip-width apart and press your thighbones backwards. As you inhale, imagine filling up your back with your breath; as you exhale, think of letting your belly hollow out while drawing the front of your rib cage toward your spine. Stay here for 5 breaths.

3. Anjaneyasana (Low Lunge)

Step your right foot forward between your hands, making sure your front knee is directly above your ankle.

Release your back knee and foot to the ground, and square your hips to face forward. On an inhalation, raise your arms toward the ceiling, palms facing one another; on an exhalation, softly draw your lower abdomen in and up. You should feel a lifting sensation in this pose. Hold for 5 deep breaths, then return to Downward-Facing Dog. Repeat on the other side.

4. Urdhva Mukha Svanasana (Upward-Facing Dog Pose)

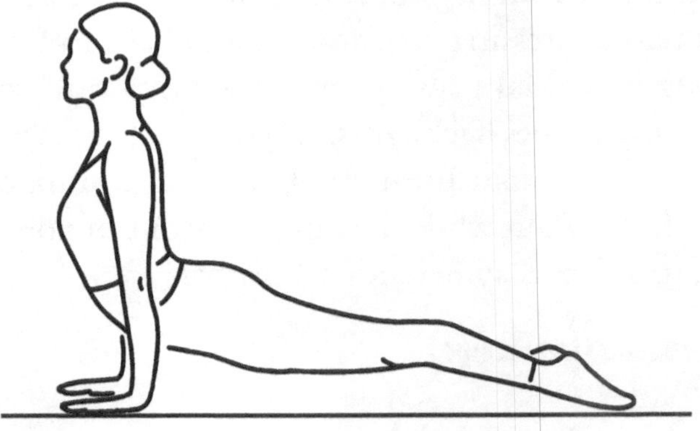

From Down Dog, shift forward to Plank Pose on an inhalation. Make sure your wrists are above your shoulders and your heels are pressing toward the back of your mat. On an exhalation, shift forward, draw in your abdomen, and lower about halfway down for Chaturanga Dandasana (Four-Limbed Staff Pose). From here, extend your arms, and allow your hips to lower. Roll onto the tops of your feet. Feel your rib cage move forward and up as you lift and open your chest; feel your shoulder blades move down your back toward one another. Take 2–3 breaths here. On an exhalation, roll over your toes and press back to Downward-Facing Dog.

5. Utthita Trikonasana (Extended Triangle Pose)

From a standing position with the legs 3 feet apart, turn the right toes to the right side and the left toes slightly inwards. Inhale and press the left hips out to the left as you slide both arms to the right parallel to the floor. Exhale and rotate only the arms, raising the left arm up and resting the right hand against the right leg, with the palms facing forward. Press into the feet, pull up the knee caps, keeping the legs strong. Reach the fingertips away from each other, bringing the arms into one straight line with the shoulders stacked on top of each other. Press the left hip forward and the right hip back. Breathe and hold for 3-6 breaths. To release, inhale and reach the raised hand up towards the ceiling as you press down into the feet using the whole body to lift back into 5 pointed star. Repeat on the other side.

6. Vasisthasana (Side Plank Pose)

On an inhalation, step back to Plank Pose, bringing your feet together to touch. On an exhalation, shift your weight to your left hand. Flex both feet, balancing on the outer edge of your left foot. Inhale, and extend your right arm skyward, directly above your shoulder. To deepen the pose, extend your top arm toward the front of the room with your palm facing down, creating a bow-like shape with your body. Take 5 breaths here, then return to Down Dog. Repeat poses 7-8 on the other side, then move through a vinyasa or into Down Dog.

7. Dolphin Pose

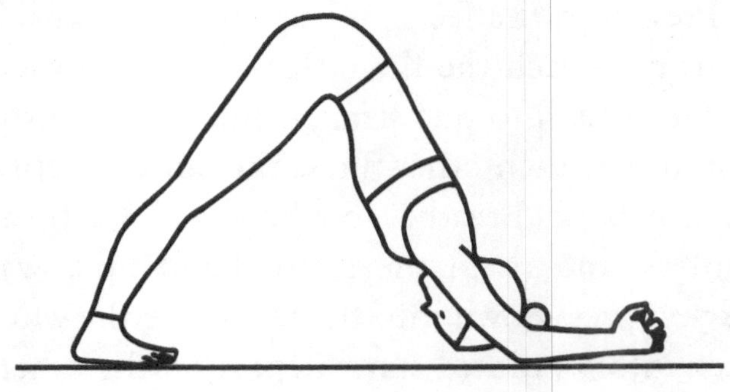

From Down Dog, come down to your hands and knees; then place your forearms on the ground, parallel, with your elbows beneath your shoulders. Press your palms firmly into your mat, tuck your toes under, and press your hips up and back to extend your legs. To emphasize the opening of your upper back and shoulders, continuously press your chest back toward your thighs while relaxing your head down toward the floor. It's OK if your heels don't reach the ground; the naturally occurring shortened angle of your hips in this posture will be more difficult on your hamstrings. Stay here for 5–8 breaths, then rest in Child's Pose.

8. Setu Bandha Sarvangasana (Bridge Pose)

Roll up and sit on your heels. Swing your legs around so they face the front of your mat, then lie down on your back. Bend your knees, plant your feet hip-width apart, and walk your heels in close to your butt. Walk your shoulders away from your ears to create a long neck. As you inhale, press into your feet to lift your hips, hugging your inner thighs toward one another. On an exhalation, walk your arms toward one another and clasp your hands underneath your back. On your next inhalation, fully press your hips up toward the ceiling, and lengthen your tailbone toward your knees. Hold here for 5 even breaths. Then, unclasp your hands, and roll your spine down to the mat.

9. Urdhva Dhanurasana (Upward Bow Pose or Wheel Pose)

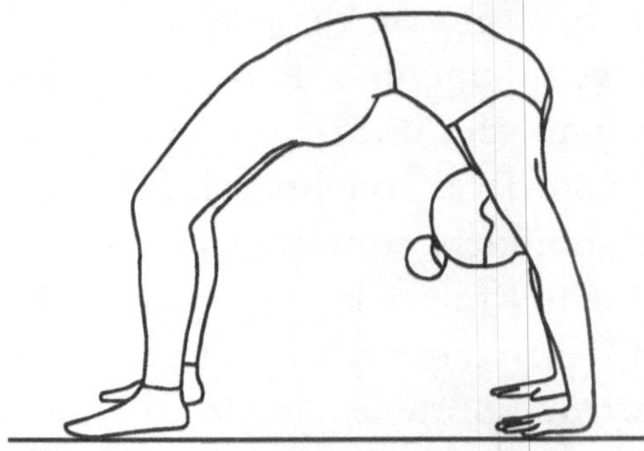

With your feet hip-width apart, heels close to your butt, place your palms down with your fingertips touching your shoulders. Hug your elbows in toward one another. Then on an inhalation, press into your hands and feet simultaneously to lift yourself up, resting the crown of your head on your mat. On your next exhalation, fully extend your arms, this time lifting the crown of your head off the floor. Take 5 deep breaths here, and at the bottom of your last exhalation, slowly tuck your chin to your chest and lower yourself back down to your mat.

10. Jathara Parivartanasana (Revolved Abdomen Pose)

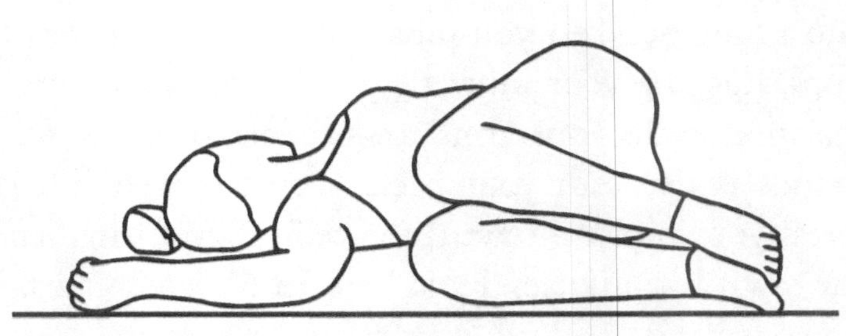

Take your feet off the mat by bringing your knees directly above your hips. Place your hands on your kneecaps and start to make gentle circles (with your knees together) in one direction 5-10 times. When you're done, bring your knees back to center above your hips, and place your arms in a cactus shape on your mat with your elbows bent. Lift your hips and move them 1-2 inches to the left, then allow your knees to gently fall to your right, keeping them level with your hips. Stay here for 1 minute, then repeat on the other side. Once you're finished, gently hug your knees into your chest.

11. Savasana (Corpse Pose)

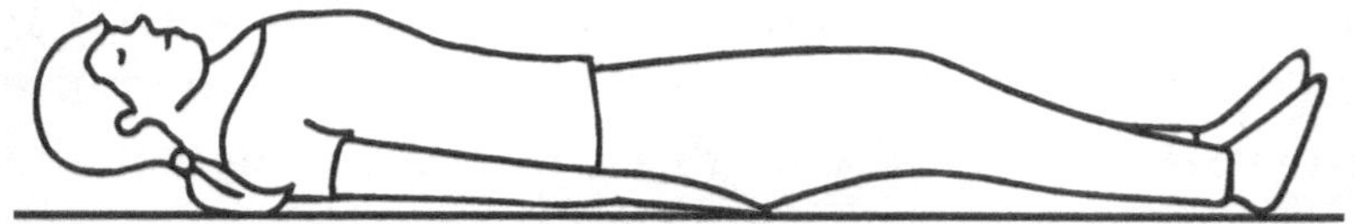

As you rest on your back, breathe naturally. Place your arms by your sides, palms facing up (which rests the shoulders), and allow your feet to splay apart. Close your eyes, and direct your attention inward. Observe where you feel warmth and energy freely flowing through your body. Observe the natural ease in your breath from all of the newfound space created in your chest and rib cage. Notice any emotions that come to the surface after opening your front body—and your heart. Breathe into the newfound space in your heart, filling yourself up with your own loving energy. Rest here for 5-7 minutes, or until you feel completely relaxed.

Yoga enables you to work on your mind, body and spirit. And when you work on them, there's no stopping you from achieving the best version of yourself, a confident YOU! But the question remains, how? The answer is simply to be found in what it teaches you. An erect spine and steady posture are accompanied by many other things when you practice yoga. You learn:

1. Focusing on your breath.

Stopping for a moment and focusing on the breath allows you to drop into the present moment. It allows you to connect with a life force that keeps you alive daily without you ever having to remind it to do its job. It distracts you from the noise of life and helps you connect with yourself. Breathwork is powerful, and it's a great tool to help you think and navigate through the ups and downs of life.

2. Everything you need is within.

While doing yoga you have lots of time to reflect. You will be able to connect more with the true version of yourself and tap into your inner strength, knowledge and power.

3. Will to push yourself out of your comfort zone.

Yoga forces you to expand yourself beyond your inner limitations. Watching your body becoming stronger and more balanced will show you what you are capable of and will improve your self-image and self-confidence, which you can achieve whatever you put your mind to.

4. Soar your emotions.

Practising yoga will give you strength and put you in a positive mood. You will be in control of your energy, if you see it dipping in the day give yourself a boost with the yoga poses mentioned in the book to boost your state of being.

"If we all did the things we are capable of doing, we would literally astound ourselves."

—*Thomas Edison*

8
Conclusion

When you lack confidence in one part of your life, it can feel like you simply aren't a confident person. We embrace our limiting beliefs as reality and fill ourselves with insecurity and doubt. Low confidence trains us to believe untruths about ourselves, and the powerful negative feelings of failure, embarrassment, or shame, make us wary of a potential emotional hazard. The feelings of low confidence don't define you or your essential worth. Everyone lacks confidence from time to time, and most people have pockets of insecurities that hold them back in certain parts of their lives.

But remember, you don't have to be perfect to be successful, happy, and confident. Confidence is a state of mind that allows you to accept failures and flaws, move past them, and to even learn from them. Confidence is a skill you can learn, practice, and improve over time, just like any other skill. When you practice confident actions and thoughts repeatedly, you will eventually feel confident. As your confidence grows, insecurity and self-doubt will vanish and have much less power over your thoughts, emotions, and actions.

If you accept the premise that change is possible, and that you can learn the skills of confidence, then begin taking some of the small steps outlined in this book to reinforce your confidence. In manageable increments, expose yourself to the things you fear. Decide on the actions you will take in the next few weeks related to the areas where you lack confidence and commit to yourself and others that you will follow through. Of course, you will feel insecure and uncomfortable at first, but the more you practice these actions, the easier it will become. If you remain committed and diligent, you will notice an improvement in your feelings of confidence. The more you work at it, the stronger those feelings of confidence will be.

"To change one's life: Start immediately. Do it flamboyantly. No exceptions. No excuses."

—William James